TITANIC HIT AN ICEBERG!

ICEBERGS vs. GLACIERS

KNOWING THE DIFFERENCE

GEOLOGY BOOKS FOR KIDS

Children's Earth Sciences Books

BABY PROFESSOR

EDUCATION KIDS

Speedy Publishing LLC
40 E. Main St. #1156
Newark, DE 19711
www.speedypublishing.com

Frozen water is ice. It lives in your freezer as ice cubes, and it covers parts of the world as glaciers. A lot of it also floats in the ocean as icebergs! Read on and learn about glaciers and icebergs!

Hubbard Glacier in Alaska.

A FROZEN RIVER

A glacier starts as snow falling. And more snow falls on top of that, year after year, without any warm seasons to melt the snow. This happens high up in mountains and at the North and South Poles, where the snow doesn't all melt even in summer.

As the layers of snow build up, they slowly compress. Over time the compressed snow turns into a mass of ice.

Glaciers are huge, and they are also on the move. Like liquid water, glaciers head down toward sea level until a land barrier gets in the way. Glaciers flow slowly, usually no more than fifty feet a day, but they are still always moving.

Ancient glacial ice.

Rappelling into a glacial ice cave.

COVERING THE EARTH

Glaciers cover about 10% of the Earth's land area, with most of the glaciers in Greenland, Antarctica, and Arctic Canada. But in the last Ice Age glaciers covered a third of the land and almost a third of the oceans.

Ice Ages happen when the Earth's temperatures get cool and stay that way for long enough for the ice at the poles to advance toward the equator. In the most recent Ice Age, glacial sheets covered most of Canada, all of New England, northwestern Russia, and much of northern Europe.

Near most glaciers you can see signs that the glacier was once much bigger, like marks on the walls of cliffs, huge fields of stones that the glacier has carried that far and then dropped when it melted and withdrew.

Grey Glacier in the Southern Patagonian Ice Field.

There have been eight Ice Ages in the last 750,000 years, separated by warming periods. Our current warming period is due to end about a thousand years from now, but changes in Earth's climate due to global warming may upset that rhythm. Read the Baby Professor book *What Every Child Should Know About Climate Change* to learn about the changes to our climate.

Melting Glacier in a Global Warming Environment

COOL GLACIER FACTS

SHAPING THE EARTH

As glaciers move out of the polar regions and down mountain ranges during Ice Ages, they carve the land. Without glaciers, we would not have fjords in Scandinavia or the Great Lakes in North America. The fertile soil that grows crops so well in the mid-western United States was carried there from Canada by glaciers.

MINIMUM SIZE

To be counted as a glacier, the body of ice has to be at least 25 acres in size. That's about the size of 20 football fields.

THE BIGGEST GLACIER

The Lambert glacier in Antarctica is about 270 miles long and over 60 miles wide.

WHERE THE FRESH WATER IS

Glaciers hold almost 70% of the Earth's fresh water. Lakes, rivers, and swamps, on the other hand, hold no more than 0.3% of the world's fresh water.

   If all that ice melted, the sea levels around the world would rise by over 260 feet. That means that cities like New York, Tokyo, London, and Los Angeles would be deep under water!

Glacier ice cave of Iceland.

TWO TYPES OF GLACIERS

Alpine glaciers are the smaller type. They flow down through mountain valleys. Continental glaciers are much larger, much broader, and don't need to find a valley to get past or over most mountain ranges.

Glacier surface.

Glacier Calving - Natural Phenomenon.

A FLOATING MOUNTAIN

Icebergs are the children of glaciers. When a tongue of a glacier reaches out into salt water, eventually the tip of it will break off and form an iceberg. This is known as *"calving"*.

ICEBERG SIZE

Small icebergs, called *"growlers"*, are about the size of a car. The next size up, about the size of a house, are sometimes called *"bergy bits"*!

There are three more size classes for icebergs. The biggest iceberg recorded so far reached 550 feet above sea level. Since most of an iceberg is under the surface of the ocean, the full height of that iceberg would have been about the size of a sixty-story building.

Large tabular iceberg floating in Antarctica.

In 2000, Iceberg B-15 calved in Antarctica. It was a half mile thick and covered an area about the size of the state of Connecticut.

ICEBERG SHAPES

Scientists group icebergs according to their shape:

- Tabular icebergs have a simple outline like a table, with steep sides and a flat top.

- Icebergs with shapes ranging from pyramids to blocks, from pillars to domes, are called non-tabular.

Broken Antarctic Iceberg off Portal Point.

ICEBERG COLORS

Most icebergs look white, but some can look blue or green. Most of the time, iceberg ice is full of air bubbles that scatter the light that hits them across all visual wavelengths. This generates white light.

However, if the ice is old and compressed, the air bubbles have been squeezed out of it. When light hits this ice the ice reflects and refracts most light waves in the blue range.

Newfoundland Turquoise Iceberg.

Often there is a layer of algae on the bottom of icebergs. When the iceberg rolls and brings to the surface what used to be deep in the water, stripes of green algae can appear.

Rippled underwater ice.

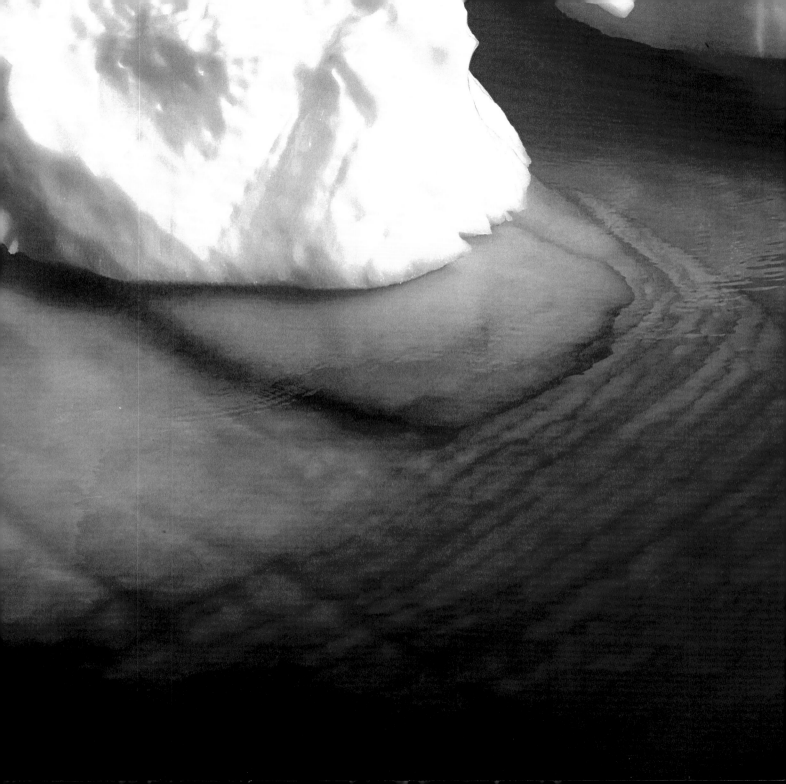

Iceberg in Antarctica.

WHY ICEBERGS FLOAT

An object floats when its density is lower than the density of the liquid it is in. Density is the mass, or amount, of material divided by the volume the material is in, or D=M/V.

Basically, density is a description of how close together the object's atoms are packed. Low-density objects have atoms spaced a distance apart from each other, while in high-density objects the separation between atoms is much smaller.

Pure liquid water has a density of 1.0 g/mL (grams per milliliter). Gold, by comparison, has a density of 19.3 g/mL, so a lump of gold will sink when you put it in water.

When water freezes and becomes ice, the water molecules move apart and form a crystalline structure. Since water expands when it freezes, the same mass takes up a greater volume. So the density of frozen water, 0.92 g/mL, is less than the 1.0 g/mL of liquid water. The result is that ice tends to float in water.

Underwater view of iceberg with beautiful transparent sea.

Visit

BABY PROFESSOR
EDUCATION KIDS

www.BabyProfessorBooks.com

to download Free Baby Professor eBooks
and view our catalog of new and exciting
Children's Books

Made in the USA
San Bernardino, CA
20 December 2017